Dire Wolf

by Julie Murray

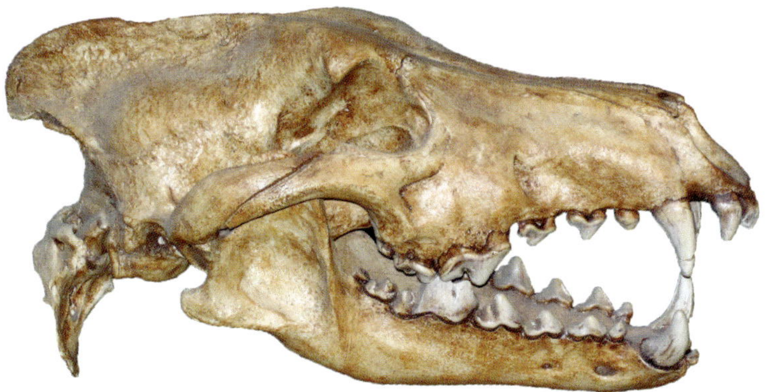

Abdo Kids Jumbo is an Imprint of Abdo Kids
abdobooks.com

abdobooks.com

Published by Abdo Kids, a division of ABDO, P.O. Box 398166, Minneapolis, Minnesota 55439.

Abdo Kids Jumbo™ is a trademark and logo of Abdo Kids.

Printed in the United States of America, North Mankato, Minnesota.

052023

092023

Photo Credits: Getty Images, Look and Learn, Science Source, Shutterstock, ©James St. John p.1,17 / CC BY 2.0, ©Mariomassone & Momotarou2012 p.11/ CC BY-SA 3.0

Production Contributors: Teddy Borth, Jennie Forsberg, Grace Hansen
Design Contributors: Candice Keimig, Pakou Moua

Library of Congress Control Number: 2022946805

Publisher's Cataloging-in-Publication Data

Names: Murray, Julie, author.

Title: Dire wolf / by Julie Murray

Description: Minneapolis, Minnesota : Abdo Kids, 2024 | Series: Ice age animals | Includes online resources and index.

Identifiers: ISBN 9781098266332 (lib. bdg.) | ISBN 9781098267032 (ebook) | ISBN 9781098267384 (Read-to-me ebook)

Subjects: LCSH: Animals--Juvenile literature. | Extinct animals--Juvenile literature. | Ice Age--Juvenile literature. | Paleontology--Juvenile literature. | Zoology--Juvenile literature.

Classification: DDC 569--dc23

Table of Contents

Ice Age

An ice age is a period when most of the Earth is covered in sheets of ice. The last ice age began about 100,000 years ago. It lasted until about 12,000 years ago. Some animals became **extinct** during this time in history.

ice
land
woolly mammoth

Dire Wolf

The dire wolf is related to modern gray wolves. It first appeared around 250,000 years ago! It lived in North America, South America, and east Asia.

Asia
North America
South America
N
W
E
S

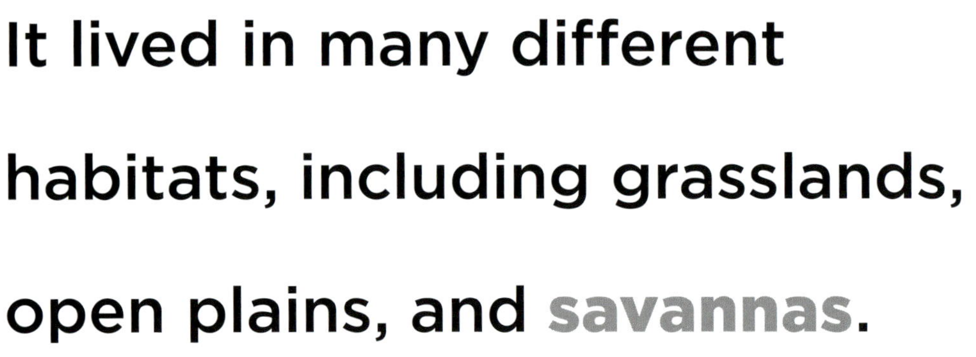

It lived in many different habitats, including grasslands, open plains, and **savannas**.

The dire wolf was bigger than modern gray wolves. It stood 3 feet (0.91 m) tall. It was 6 feet (1.8 m) long. It could weigh 150 pounds (68 kg).

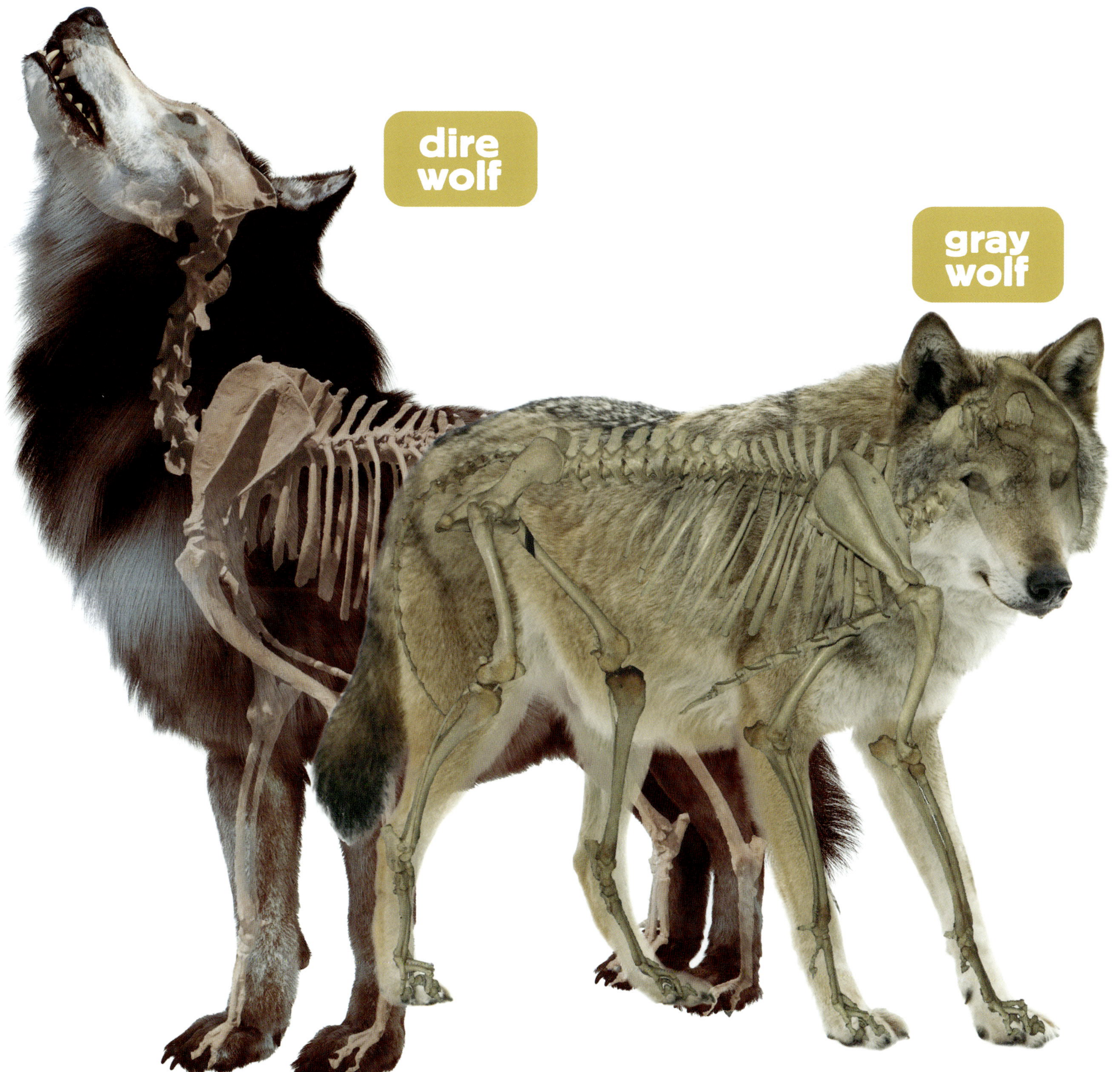
dire wolf
gray wolf

It had reddish brown fur. Its legs were short and its body was thick. It had a long, bushy tail.

Hunting and Food

Dire wolves lived with, hunted, and traveled in packs. A pack could have up to 30 wolves.

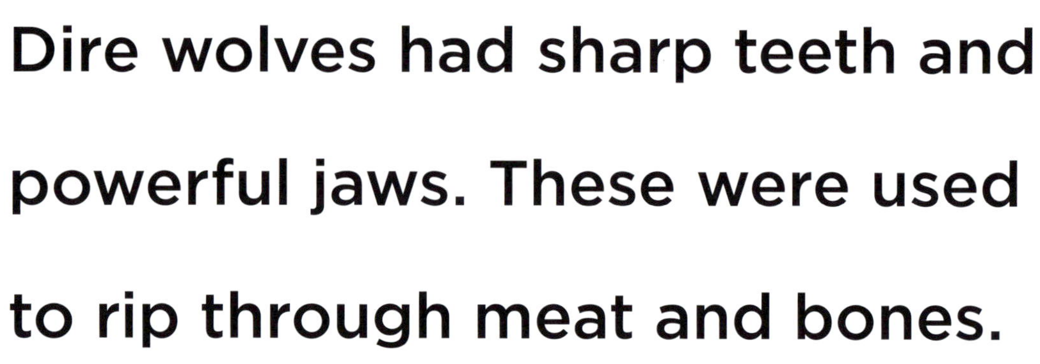

Dire wolves had sharp teeth and powerful jaws. These were used to rip through meat and bones.

Dire wolves mainly ate the meat of large animals, including bison, wild horses, and mastodons.

Extinction

The dire wolf went **extinct** about 13,000 years ago. Its **prey** significantly declined around this time. Without food to eat, the dire wolf could not survive.

More Facts

- The first dire wolf **fossils** were found in 1854. Francis Lincke discovered them near Evansville, Indiana.
- The Rancho La Brea Tar Pits are in Los Angeles, California. Thousands of dire wolf fossils have been found there. A total of 400 skulls are on display at the National History Museum of Los Angeles County.
- *Dire* means fearsome or frightful. The dire wolf lived up to its name. It was a **fierce** hunter with a bone-crushing bite!

Glossary

extinct – no longer existing.

fierce – wild and dangerous.

fossil – the remains or trace of a living animal or plant from a long time ago.

prey – an animal that is hunted by other animals for food.

savanna – a flat plain covered with grass that also has scattered trees. Found in Africa and other tropical regions.

Index

Visit **abdokids.com** to access crafts, games, videos, and more!

Use Abdo Kids code

IDK6332

or scan this QR code!